MW01527520

ANNE OF GREEN TOMATOES

The Right to be Safe and Secure

Written by Dustin Milligan • Illustrated by Jasmine Vicente

DC Canada Education Publishing

Written by: Dustin Milligan

Illustrated by: Jasmine Vicente

Editor: Leonard Judge

Copy Editor: Anja Pujic

Cover Design: Meredith Luce

Published in 2012 by: DC Canada Education Publishing

180 Metcalfe Street, Suite 204
Ottawa, On, Canada K2P 1P5
www.dc-canada.ca

· ·

Text © 2012 Dustin Milligan
Illustrations © 2012 DC Canada Education Publishing

Printed in Canada

10 9 8 7 6 5 4 3 2

All rights reserved. No part of this book may be reproduced
in any form or by any electronic or mechanical
means including information storage and retrieval systems
without written permission of the copyright owner.

We acknowledge the financial support of the Government of Canada
through the Canada Book Fund for our publishing activities.

Anne of Green Tomatoes

ISBN: 978-1-926776-43-9

· ·

Library and Archives Canada Cataloguing in Publication

Milligan, Dustin, 1984-

Anne of Green Tomatoes : the right to be safe and secure /
written by Dustin Milligan ; illustrated by Jasmine Vicente.

(The charter for children)

Includes bibliographical references.

ISBN 978-1-926776-43-9

1. Human security--Canada--Juvenile literature.

I. Vicente, Jasmine II. Title. III. Series: Charter for children

JC571.M55 2012   j323.4'30971   C2012-901832-5

Preface

The idea for *The Charter for Children* first emerged when I was a student at the Faculty of Law at McGill University. After my first year of studies, I was concerned that the common citizen wasn't equipped to understand our country's complicated legal system—one that I myself had only begun to comprehend. Children are at a further disadvantage in this regard, as they have limited capacity, strength and knowledge of their rights. Combining these concerns with my love for literature and the law, I took on this large project—writing a series of books that offer children a basic understanding of the *Canadian Charter of Rights and Freedoms*. Thus *The Charter for Children* was born.

I would like to thank the Faculty of Law of McGill University, and most notably, Professor Shauna Van Praagh, who provided guidance during the course of much of this project and without whom the project would not have been possible. I would also like to thank those who have contributed their thoughts, insights, encouragement, time and puns—most notably, my three friends, Dorian Needham, Malcolm Dort and Josie Marks, as well as the wonderful team at DC Canada Education Publishing, Jeannine Plamondon, Professor Tina Piper, Georgina Murphy, Megan Reid, Meagan Johnston, Megan Howatt, and my incredible family, Keith, Deborah, Olivia, Christian and Jolene.

This series is dedicated to the children of Canada—may your voices be heard and considered, and may your childhoods be filled with respect and dignity.

Dustin Milligan

**The opinions and views expressed in this
book do not reflect those of the public figures
or entities referred to or parodied in this story.**

In a time not so long ago, in the gardens of Leamington, Ontario, there lived a green tomato named Anne.

Anne loved reading and had a huge imagination. She always had her stem in a book.

Her favourite authors were Yam Martel and Gabrielle Pois. She bought their latest books from the market at the end of the garden.

On her way home, she started reading one of the new books, *Life of Pea*.

Anne had also written many stories. She dreamed of becoming an author.

She had just completed two stories called *The English Parsnip* and *The Blind Asparagus*.

Her latest story was going to be an autobiography. She was going to call it *Anne of Green Tomatoes*.

Just like in the books that Anne read, there was a troubled plot in the gardens of Leamington.

The veggieslature, which governed Leamington, displayed a large basket of red tomatoes in the market each day.

Every morning, the red tomatoes arrived at the market and jumped into the basket to show off their beauty. But sometimes, there weren't enough red tomatoes to fill the basket.

When there weren't enough red tomatoes, a guard from the veggieslature searched the garden rows of Leamington for green tomatoes. When he found a green tomato, he used a giant brush to cover the green tomato in red paint!

The painted tomatoes were then taken to the market. They were put at the bottom of the basket to hold the red tomatoes up higher for display.

One Saturday, Anne sat quietly in the middle of the vegetable rows writing her latest story.

She was trying to describe what Anne of Green Tomatoes looked like. She wrote:

Anne wore a straw hat with spinach wrapped around,
And two red carrots picked freshly from the ground!

As Anne's imagination flourished, the guard found her. He took his giant paintbrush and painted Anne red.

Anne was taken to the market. She was placed at the bottom of the basket of tomatoes.

The basket looked beautiful, full of many bright red tomatoes.

But all day long, Anne felt sick with the red paint on her skin and she hated being squished at the bottom of the basket.

When she got home that night, Anne washed the red paint off her skin with the garden hose.

She felt ill. She had bruises from being on the bottom of the pile all day.

With an ache in her seeds, she climbed up her vine and went directly to bed.

As Anne tried to fall asleep, the nightmares began. Every time she closed her eyes, she dreamed of the purple guard and his paintbrush dripping with red paint!

Anne tossed and turned all night long. By the next morning, her head was pounding. She felt awful.

Her father climbed up the vine. He put a bag of frozen peas on her head and asked:

What is wrong my dearest tomato?
You look like you ate a rotten potato.
Do you have pains in your seeds?
Did you fight with one of the weeds?

Anne couldn't respond. She simply moaned. She spent the entire day in bed.

The next day, Anne was feeling a little better. She decided to go for a walk between the rows of tomatoes. As she strolled through the garden, she tried to imagine Anne of Green Tomatoes. But she was too scared to concentrate.

All she could think about was the guard chasing her with a giant paintbrush!

The more she imagined, the bigger the guard became—taller even than the CN Tower!

Anne needed to escape. She needed to hide. She started running down the long row of vegetables.

But the faster she ran, the closer the paintbrush came to her skin. The paint was flowing from the guard's brush like the water at Niagara Falls!

Anne ran through row upon row of the garden.

She screamed:

Help! Help! He's going to paint me red!
I'll be dead! Dead! Or sick and bruised in my bed!

Just when she thought she had lost the guard, Anne's imagination ran wild!

She found herself in a dark row. A large patch of sunflowers stood in her way.

The guard, with his large bucket of red paint, entered the dark row with an evil grin.

She was trapped!

Anne shook her head. "It's not real," she told herself.

Too scared to be in the garden alone, she ran to see her friend Diane. Diane asked her what was wrong.

Anne said:

> *My kindred tomato, I feel ill as old dill.*
> *I was painted red by the eggplant on the hill!*
> *I'm more scared than Franklin in the Dark.*
> *Let's both run away to Point Pelee Park!*

Anne learned that Diane had also been painted red for the market.

Diane replied:

We cannot run away or turn a blind eye.
We must search for a way to hold our stems high!
Let's think of a plan, my dear friend Anne,
Over bowls of ice cream and alligator pie!

That night, Anne and Diane let their creativity shine. They wanted to do something to ensure that all green tomatoes felt safe in the gardens of Leamington.

Anne said:

Maybe we can dress like paper bag princesses?
And save our prince veggies from all their distresses?

Diane said:

Or maybe hire Superyam, that sweet potato in blue tights,
He can fly down from the sky and save us from our plights!

After discussing the possibilities all night, Anne and Diane developed a plan.

When they awoke the next morning, they went to visit the sunflowers. The sunflowers were already hot and sweaty from the bright morning sun.

Anne and Diane held jars beneath the sunflowers' petals. They collected jars and jars of sunflower oil.

Anne said:

> *Dearest sunflowers, thanks for your oil.*
> *We're fighting for justice upon this soil!*
> *Our bodies and skins are our very own.*
> *And green tomatoes must be left alone!*

Anne and Diane delivered a jar of sunflower oil to every green tomato in the garden.

Together, they would protect their bodies and skins.

As Anne and Diane handed out the jars, they said to the green tomatoes:

We have the right to feel secure!
The veggieslature must ensure,
That our bodies are safe from stem to toe,
So that upon this soil we can grow!

The next morning, the guard searched the garden for green tomatoes, as usual.

This time, he found many green tomatoes out in the open. None were hiding.

Anne and Diane stood right in the centre of Main Row. It was the busiest row in the garden.

They laughed and giggled like kindred tomatoes do.

The guard approached Anne. But Anne did not run. She stood there as the guard took his large paintbrush and tried to paint her red.

But the paint slipped off!

Anne said:

> We have the right to feel secure!
> The veggieslature must ensure,
> That our bodies are safe from stem to toe,
> So that upon this soil we can grow!

As the guard tried brushing her again, Anne imagined that she was Captain Canuck fighting her evil enemy!

The guard was angry. He took another dip of paint and brushed Diane.

Diane said:

Our bodies and minds deserve respect!
The veggieslature must protect,
Our skins and seeds from stem to toe,
So that upon this soil we can grow!

Every drop of paint slipped off their slick, green skins.

The guard was in shock. He tried to paint every green tomato in the garden. But every time he tried, the paint slipped off.

And each tomato said:

> *We have the right to feel secure!*
> *The veggieslature must ensure,*
> *That our bodies are safe from stem to toe,*
> *So that upon this soil we can grow!*

The green tomatoes had put sunflower oil on their skins. The paint would no longer stick.

And that day, for the first time in a long time, all the green tomatoes played freely in the garden.

They were all out in the rows, playing hide and ketch-up or reading books beneath their vines.

They basked in the sun parlour of Canada! They finally felt safe and secure.

At the market, the veggieslature learned to do without the green tomatoes.

With the new respect for the bodies and skins of the green tomatoes, the tomatoes grew red faster.

When asked, the guard said:

Green tomatoes must be safe and secure,
To feel healthy and become mature.
The beauty of the basket is no excuse,
For illness, or sadness, or emotional abuse!

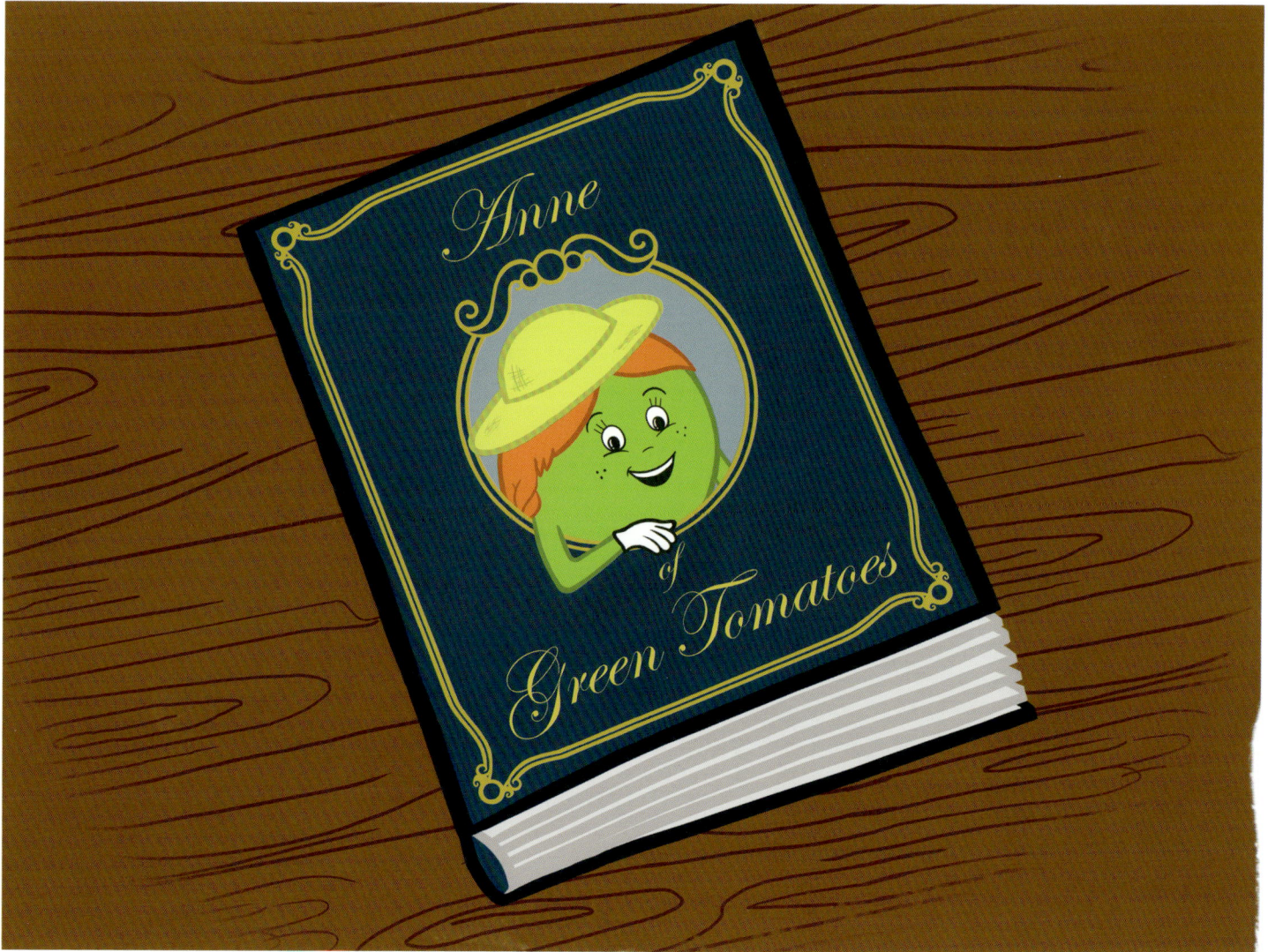

And with her imagination restored, Anne finished the next chapter of *Anne of Green Tomatoes*.

It went like this:

> *Anne fought the guard just like a knight,*
> *She fought for what's fair and what's right!*
> *She drew her sword, the guard then fled!*
> *With armour of squash, she then said,*
> *"Green tomatoes have a right to feel,*
> *Secure in their bodies, minds, and peels!"*

It was, indeed, a storybook ending.

Note for Parents and Teachers:

This story seeks to teach children about the right to security of the person, which is guaranteed by section 7 of the *Canadian Charter of Rights and Freedoms*. This section provides that:

> *Everyone has the right to life, liberty, and security of the person and the right not to be deprived thereof except in accordance with the principles of fundamental justice.*[1]

Whereas the *Criminal Code of Canada* protects people against bodily harm caused by other individuals, the Charter right to "security of the person" protects individuals against bodily harm caused by policies or actions of the government (for example, by state actors such as law enforcement officers).

The right applies to both physical and psychological harm. Physically, the right to "security of the person" prohibits the government from interfering with an individual's bodily integrity. Psychologically, it guarantees individuals freedom from serious state-imposed psychological or emotional stress.[2]

In this story, the guard for the veggieslature (a state actor) interferes with both the physical and the psychological components of security of the person by painting the green tomatoes red. Anne's bruises and illness represent the physical component. Anne's loss of imagination and mental stress represent the psychological component.

Anne and Diane overcome the infringement of their personal security by covering themselves in sunflower oil. As the paint slips off the green tomatoes, the veggieslature is forced to change its practice of painting green tomatoes red. The veggieslature finally realizes that the beauty of the basket does not justify the serious harm done to the green tomatoes. In the end, the community realizes that the green tomatoes can grow faster (or, turn red quicker) when their physical and psychological security are protected.

Questions for children:

1. How did Anne feel after she was painted red? Did Diane and the other green tomatoes feel the same way?

2. Why did the guard paint the green tomatoes red? Was it right for the guard to paint the green tomatoes red?

3. At the end of the story, we find out that the green tomatoes grow faster when they aren't scared of being painted red. Why do you think this makes them grow faster?

¹ *Canadian Charter of Rights and Freedoms*, s 7, Part I of the *Constitution Act, 1982*, being Schedule B to the *Canada Act 1982* (UK), 1982, c 11.

² *Rodriguez v British Columbia* (AG), [1993] 3 SCR 519, 107 DLR (4th) 342.